# REIMS TRAVEL GUIDE 2024

Explore the City of Kings and Champagne

**ALEXANDER PAUL**

**Copyright© 2024 ALEXANDER PAUL**

All rights reserved.
No part of this book may be reproduced, stored in a retrieval
system, or transmitted in any form or by any means,
electronic, mechanical, photocopying, recording, or otherwise,
without the prior written permission of the publisher.
Unauthorized reproduction of this book, or parts thereof, is
prohibited by law and may result in legal action

# Table of Contents

| | |
|---|---|
| **Chapter 1: Introduction to Reims** | **13** |
| Unveiling the Heart of Champagne | 15 |
| A Glimpse into Reims' History | 15 |
| Notre-Dame de Reims Cathedral | 16 |
| Palace of Tau | 17 |
| What Makes Reims a Must-Visit in 2024 | 18 |
| The Champagne Experience | 18 |
| Taittinger Champagne House | 19 |
| Veuve Clicquot Ponsardin | 19 |
| Cultural Vibrancy | 20 |
| Museum of Fine Arts | 20 |
| Reims Opera House | 20 |
| A Gastronomic Haven | 21 |
| L'Assiette Champenoise | 21 |
| Le Bocal | 22 |
| Events and Festivals | 22 |
| Practical Information for Visitors | 23 |
| Reims Tourist Information Center | 23 |
| Emergency Contacts | 23 |
| **Chapter 2: Getting to Reims** | **24** |
| Flying In: Nearest Airports | 24 |
| Paris Charles de Gaulle Airport (CDG) | 25 |
| Paris Orly Airport (ORY) | 25 |
| Brussels Airport (BRU) | 26 |
| All Aboard: Train Travel Options | 26 |
| TER (Transport Express Régional) | 28 |

| | |
|---|---|
| Road Trips: Driving Routes | 28 |
| Public Transit: Buses and Trams | 29 |
| Bus Services: | 29 |
| **Chapter 3: Navigating Reims** | **32** |
| Walking Routes Through Historic Quarters | 33 |
| Explore the Cathedral Quarter | 33 |
| Stroll Along Rue de Vesle | 33 |
| Discover Place Drouet d'Erlon | 33 |
| Cycling the City Streets | 34 |
| VéloCité Bike-Sharing System | 34 |
| Scenic Cycling Routes | 34 |
| Getting Around by Taxi and Rental Car | 35 |
| Taxi Services | 35 |
| Parking in Reims | 35 |
| **Chapter 4: Where to Stay inReims** | **37** |
| Luxury Retreats: High-End Hotels | 37 |
| L'Assiette Champenoise Hotel | 37 |
| Château Les Crayères | 38 |
| Comfortable Stays: Mid-Range Accommodations | 39 |
| Hotel Continental Centre Ville | 39 |
| Novotel Suites Reims Centre | 39 |
| Budget-Friendly Options | 40 |
| Ibis Budget Reims Centre | 40 |
| Hostellerie La Briqueterie | 40 |
| Unique and Boutique Hotels | 41 |
| Hotel de la Paix | 41 |
| Grand Hotel des Templiers | 41 |
| **Chapter 5: Top Attractions in Reims** | **43** |
| Majestic Reims Cathedral | 43 |

| | |
|---|---|
| Notre-Dame de Reims Cathedral | 43 |
| Historical Treasures: Palais du Tau and Saint Remi Basilica | 44 |
| Palais du Tau | 44 |
| Saint Remi Basilica | 45 |
| Champagne Houses and Tastings | 46 |
| Taittinger Champagne House | 46 |
| Veuve Clicquot Ponsardin | 47 |
| Museums of Art and History | 48 |
| Museum of Fine Arts | 48 |
| Musée de la Reddition (Surrender Museum) | 49 |
| **Chapter 6: Exploring Reims' Districts** | **51** |
| Old Town Charms: Centre-Ville | 51 |
| Place Drouet d'Erlon | 51 |
| Artistic Vibes: Quartier Boulingri | 52 |
| Marché du Boulingrin | 52 |
| Riverside Serenity: Quartier des Capucins | 53 |
| Promenade de la Suippe | 53 |
| Historic Bridges | 54 |
| **Chapter 7: Immersing in Reims' Culture** | **55** |
| Art Galleries and Creative Spaces | 55 |
| FRAC Champagne-Ardenne | 55 |
| Galerie Martine Ehmer | 56 |
| Theatrical Performances and Events | 57 |
| Opéra de Reims | 57 |
| La Comédie de Reims | 58 |
| Festivals and Cultural Celebrations | 59 |
| Fêtes Johanniques | 59 |
| Festival Flâneries Musicales | 59 |

**Chapter 8: Outdoor Adventures Around Reims**     **61**

Champagne Vineyards and Tours     62

Champagne Tasting Tours     63

Recommended Tours:     63

Parks, Gardens, and Green Spaces     64

Parc de Champagne     64

Jardin des Secrets     65

Sports and Recreation Activities     66

Golf de Reims     66

Canoeing on the Marne River     66

**Chapter 9: Shopping in Reims**     **68**

Local Markets and Specialty Stores     68

Marché du Boulingrin     68

Les Halles du Boulingrin     68

Boutique Shopping and Designer Finds     69

Rue de Vesle     70

Shopping Centers for Every Need     71

Centre Commercial Espace d'Erlon     71

Parc Commercial Cernay     71

**Chapter 10: Dining and Cuisine in Reims**     **73**

Gastronomic Delights: Regional Cuisine     74

Bouchon des Filles     74

Le Foch     75

Champagne Pairings and Tastings     76

Les Crayères     76

Caves du Forum     76

Fine Dining Experiences     77

Assiette Champenoise     77

L'Alambic     78

| | |
|---|---|
| Cozy Cafés and Bistros | 78 |
| Café du Palais | 78 |
| Le Gaulois | 78 |
| **Chapter 11: Nightlife and Entertainment** | **80** |
| Bars and Pubs: Local Hotspots | 81 |
| Le Coq Rouge | 81 |
| Café du Palais | 81 |
| Nightclubs for Dancing | 81 |
| Live Music Venues | 82 |
| La Comédie de Reims | 82 |
| Le Temps des Cerises | 83 |
| Cultural Evenings and Events | 83 |
| Palais du Tau | 83 |
| Festival Flâneries Musicales de Reims | 84 |
| **Chapter 12: Day Trips from Reims** | **85** |
| Epernay: Capital of Champagne | 85 |
| Avenue de Champagne | 86 |
| Charming Villages of Montagne de Reims | 86 |
| Verzy | 86 |
| Historical Sites: Verdun and Laon | 87 |
| Verdun | 87 |
| Laon | 88 |
| **Chapter 13: Family-Friendly Activities** | **90** |
| Museums and Interactive Exhibits | 90 |
| Musée Automobile Reims-Champagne | 90 |
| Planétarium de Reims | 91 |
| Parks, Playgrounds, and Picnic Spots | 92 |
| Parc de la Patte d'Oie | 92 |
| Jardin d'Horticulture | 93 |

Educational Tours and Workshops 94

Champagne Tasting Workshops 94

Various Champagne houses in Reims 95

**Chapter 14: Practical Information for Visitors 96**

Tourist Information Centers 96

Office de Tourisme de Reims 96

Emergency Contacts 96

Emergency Services 96

Local Etiquette and Customs 97

Greetings 97

**Chapter 15: Travel Tips for Reims 99**

Best Times to Visit 100

Safety Tips and Advice 100

Budget Planning Tips 100

Eco-Friendly Travel Practices 101

**Chapter 16: Reims for Business Travelers 103**

Conference Venues and Meeting Spaces 104

Centre des Congrès de Reims 104

Domaine Pommery 104

Business Services and Amenities 105

Business Hotels 105

Hôtel de la Paix 105

Networking Opportunities 106

Reims Chamber of Commerce and Industry 106

Professional Networking Groups 106

**Chapter 17: Conclusion 108**

Reflecting on Your Reims Experience 108

Souvenirs and Memories to Take Home 108

Planning Your Return to Reims 109

# Chapter 1: Introduction to Reims

# Unveiling the Heart of Champagne

Nestled in the northeastern part of France, Reims is more than just the unofficial capital of the Champagne region; it is a city where history, culture, and viticulture intertwine to create an unforgettable destination. Often referred to as the "City of Kings," Reims is renowned for its historical significance and its pivotal role in the coronation of French monarchs. This chapter will delve into what makes Reims a must-visit destination in 2024, highlighting its rich heritage, vibrant cultural scene, and, of course, its world-famous Champagne.

## A Glimpse into Reims' History

Reims' history is as effervescent as the Champagne it produces. Founded by the Gauls and later conquered by the Romans, the city has been a witness to numerous historical events that shaped France. The most significant of these is the tradition of French kings being crowned at the Notre-Dame de Reims Cathedral, a Gothic masterpiece that stands as a testament to the city's medieval grandeur. This tradition began with Clovis I, the first King of the Franks, who was baptized here in 496 AD, establishing Reims as a sacred site of French royalty.

## Notre-Dame de Reims Cathedral

No visit to Reims is complete without a stop at the Notre Dame de Reims Cathedral. This UNESCO World Heritage site is celebrated for its stunning architecture, intricate stained-glass windows, and the famous Smiling Angel statue.

The cathedral, which took nearly a century to complete, has witnessed the coronation of 33 kings of France. In 2024, visitors can enjoy guided tours that delve into its history and marvel at the light and sound shows that bring its facade to life in the evenings.

- Address: Place du Cardinal Luçon, 51100 Reims, France
- Website: [Notre-Dame de Reims Cathedral](https://www.cathedrale-reims.com)

## Palace of Tau

Adjacent to the cathedral is the Palace of Tau, the former residence of the archbishops of Reims. This palace now serves as a museum, showcasing the rich history of the cathedral and the coronations. Here, you can find a collection of artefacts, including the original statues and tapestries from the cathedral, as well as the royal regalia used during the coronation ceremonies.

- Address: 2 Place du Cardinal Luçon, 51100 Reims, France
- Website: [Palace of Tau](http://www.palais-tau.fr)

# What Makes Reims a Must-Visit in 2024

## The Champagne Experience

Reims is synonymous with Champagne. As the largest city in the Champagne region, it serves as the perfect gateway to exploring the world of this prestigious sparkling wine. The city's underground cellars, known as "crayères," are a marvel in themselves. These ancient chalk caves, some of which date back to Roman times, provide the perfect conditions for ageing Champagne. Many of the world's most famous Champagne houses, including Veuve Clicquot, Pommery, and Taittinger, offer tours and tastings, giving visitors an insider's look at the art of Champagne making.

## Taittinger Champagne House

A visit to the Taittinger Champagne House offers an immersive experience of the history and production of Champagne. The guided tours take you through the ancient Roman chalk pits that now serve as the cellars, followed by a tasting session of some of their finest cuvées.

- Address: 9 Place Saint-Nicaise, 51100 Reims, France
- Website: [Taittinger](https://www.taittinger.com)

## Veuve Clicquot Ponsardin

Another iconic Champagne house, Veuve Clicquot, offers an extensive tour of its cellars, where you can learn about the house's rich history and the story behind its famous yellow label. The tour concludes with a tasting of their renowned Champagnes.

- Address: 1 Place des Droits de l'Homme, 51100 Reims, France
- Website: [Veuve Clicquot](https://www.veuveclicquot.com)

## Cultural Vibrancy

Reims is not just about history and Champagne; it also boasts a vibrant cultural scene. The city is home to numerous museums, galleries, and theaters that offer a diverse array of artistic and cultural experiences.

## Museum of Fine Arts

The Museum of Fine Arts in Reims houses an impressive collection of artworks ranging from the Renaissance to modern times. Visitors can admire works by masters such as Cranach, Corot, and Pissarro, as well as a notable collection of Art Deco pieces.

- Address: 8 Rue Chanzy, 51100 Reims, France
- Website: [Museum of Fine Arts](https://musees-reims.fr/fr/musee-des-beaux-arts)

## Reims Opera House

For a taste of performing arts, the Reims Opera House offers a variety of performances, including operas, ballets, and concerts. This beautiful venue, with its opulent interiors, provides an unforgettable cultural experience.

- Address: 1 Place Myron Herrick, 51100 Reims, France
- Website: [Reims Opera House](https://www.operadereims.com)

## A Gastronomic Haven

Reims is also a haven for food lovers. The city's culinary scene ranges from traditional French bistros to Michelin-starred restaurants. Local specialties include ham of Reims, pink biscuits (biscuits roses), and, of course, dishes perfectly paired with Champagne.

## L'Assiette Champenoise

For an extraordinary dining experience, head to L'Assiette Champenoise, a three-star Michelin restaurant located just outside the city centre. Chef Arnaud Lallement offers an exquisite menu that showcases the best of French cuisine with a contemporary twist.

- Address: 40 Avenue Paul Vaillant-Couturier, 51430 Tinqueux, France
- Website: [L'Assiette Champenoise](https://www.assiettechampenoise.com)

## Le Bocal

For a more casual yet delightful meal, Le Bocal is a charming seafood restaurant known for its fresh oysters and delicious seafood platters. The relaxed atmosphere and quality of food make it a favorite among locals and visitors alike.

- Address: 31 Cours Jean-Baptiste Langlet, 51100 Reims, France
- Website: [Le Bocal](https://www.lebocalreims.fr)

## Events and Festivals

Reims hosts numerous events and festivals throughout the year, adding to its allure. One of the highlights is the Joan of Arc Festival, which celebrates the city's historical connection to the saint with parades, medieval reenactments, and fireworks.

### Joan of Arc Festival

Held annually in June, this festival commemorates Joan of Arc's role in the coronation of Charles VII at the Reims Cathedral. The event includes a grand procession, historical reenactments, and various cultural activities that bring the medieval history of Reims to life.

- Address: Various locations around Reims
- Website: [Joan of Arc Festival](https://www.reims.fr)

# Practical Information for Visitors

When planning a trip to Reims, it's essential to have practical information at hand. The city's tourist information center is an excellent resource for maps, guides, and tips on making the most of your visit.

## Reims Tourist Information Center

- Address: 6 Rue Rockefeller, 51100 Reims, France
- Website: [Reims Tourism](https://www.reims-tourism.com)

## Emergency Contacts

- Police: 17
- Medical Emergency: 15
- Fire Department: 18

Reims is a city that promises a rich tapestry of experiences, from its royal past and stunning Gothic architecture to its world-renowned Champagne houses and vibrant cultural scene. As you explore its historic streets, savor its culinary delights, and sip its finest Champagnes, you'll discover why Reims is a must-visit destination in 2024. Whether you're a history buff, a food enthusiast, or a lover of fine wine, Reims has something to offer everyone, making it a truly enchanting place to explore.

# Chapter 2: Getting to Reims

## Flying In: Nearest Airports

Reims is conveniently accessible by air, with several airports within a reasonable distance offering both domestic and international flights.

## Paris Charles de Gaulle Airport (CDG)

Located approximately 145 kilometers southwest of Reims, Paris Charles de Gaulle Airport is one of the busiest airports in Europe and serves as a major gateway to the region. From CDG, travelers can reach Reims by train, car, or shuttle services.

- Transport Options: Direct trains from CDG TGV station to Reims, with a travel time of about 45 minutes to 1 hour. Rental cars and shuttle services are also available.

## Paris Orly Airport (ORY)

Situated about 180 kilometers southwest of Reims, Paris Orly Airport is another option for travelers flying into the region.

Similar to CDG, Orly offers various transportation options to reach Reims.

- Transport Options: Trains from Paris city center to Reims, connecting via Gare de l'Est or Gare du Nord stations. Rental cars and shuttle services are also available.

## Brussels Airport (BRU)

For international travelers, Brussels Airport, located approximately 300 kilometers north of Reims, provides connections from major European cities and beyond.

- Transport Options: High-speed trains (Thalys or Eurostar) from Brussels Midi station to Paris, then transfer to Reims via train. Rental cars and shuttle services are available at the airport.

# All Aboard: Train Travel Options

### TGV (Train à Grande Vitesse)

Reims is well-connected to France's high-speed train network, making it easily accessible from major cities across the country.

- From Paris: Direct TGV trains depart from Paris Gare de l'Est to Reims, with a travel time of approximately 45 minutes to 1 hour.

- From other cities: TGV trains also connect Reims to cities like Lille, Strasbourg, Lyon, and Marseille, offering efficient and comfortable travel options.

## TER (Transport Express Régional)

Regional trains (TER) provide connections to Reims from nearby cities and towns within the Grand Est region.

- Local Connections: TER trains operate frequent services from cities like Épernay, Châlons-en-Champagne, and Charleville-Mézières, providing convenient travel options for regional visitors.

# Road Trips: Driving Routes

**From Paris:**

Reims is accessible via the A4 motorway (Autoroute de l'Est), which connects Paris directly to the city. The journey takes approximately 1.5 to 2 hours, depending on traffic conditions.

**From Brussels:**
Travelers driving from Brussels can take the E19/E42 motorway southbound, connecting to the A4/E50 near Charleroi. From there, continue on the A4 towards Reims, with a total driving time of approximately 3 to 4 hours, depending on traffic and border crossing times.

## Public Transit: Buses and Trams

### Bus Services:
Reims has an efficient local bus network operated by Citura, providing comprehensive coverage of the city and its suburbs. Buses are a convenient way to explore Reims and reach

28

various attractions, including the Champagne houses and historic sites.

- Tickets: Tickets can be purchased on board or at local ticket offices. Day passes and multi-journey tickets are available for frequent travelers.

**Tramway**:
Reims boasts a modern tramway system that connects key areas of the city, offering fast and reliable transportation for residents and visitors alike.

- Lines: The tram network consists of three lines (A, B, and C), with Line A serving the central areas and Lines B and C extending to the outskirts and neighboring towns.

**Bike Rentals:**
For eco-conscious travelers, Reims also offers a bike-sharing scheme called VéloCité, providing bicycles for short-term rental at various stations across the city.

Reims' accessibility by air, train, road, and public transit makes it a highly convenient destination for travelers exploring the Champagne region. Whether you prefer the speed of high-speed trains, the flexibility of driving, or the convenience of local buses and trams, Reims offers multiple options to suit every traveler's preferences and itinerary. Plan your journey to Reims with ease, knowing that you have a variety of transportation choices at your disposal to ensure a seamless travel experience.

# Chapter 3: Navigating Reims

# Walking Routes Through Historic Quarters

Reims, with its rich history and compact city center, is best explored on foot. Walking allows visitors to immerse themselves in the charm of its historic quarters, discovering hidden gems and iconic landmarks along the way.

## Explore the Cathedral Quarter

Begin your walking tour in the heart of Reims at the Cathedral Quarter, where the majestic Notre-Dame de Reims Cathedral dominates the skyline. Wander through Place du Cardinal Luçon and Rue Libergier, lined with quaint shops, cafés, and historical buildings. Don't miss the opportunity to admire the intricate facade of the cathedral and the nearby Palace of Tau, both UNESCO World Heritage sites.

## Stroll Along Rue de Vesle

From the Cathedral Quarter, take a leisurely stroll along Rue de Vesle, one of Reims' main shopping streets. Here, you'll find a mix of well-known brands, local boutiques, and charming bistros. This bustling street offers a vibrant atmosphere and is ideal for souvenir shopping or enjoying a coffee break.

## Discover Place Drouet d'Erlon

Continue your walk to Place Drouet d'Erlon, Reims' lively central square known for its bustling markets, street performers, and outdoor cafés. This pedestrian-friendly square is perfect for people-watching and sampling local delicacies, such as the famous pink biscuits (biscuits roses) and regional cheeses.

# Cycling the City Streets

For those who prefer cycling, Reims offers bike-friendly routes that allow you to explore the city at your own pace.

## VéloCité Bike-Sharing System

Take advantage of Reims' VéloCité bike-sharing system, which provides bicycles for rent at various stations throughout the city. With over 40 stations conveniently located, you can easily pick up and drop off bikes at your leisure.

- Rental Process: Register online or at a station terminal, choose a subscription plan (daily, weekly, or monthly), and unlock bikes using a code or card.

## Scenic Cycling Routes

Explore Reims' scenic surroundings by cycling along the Canal de l'Aisne à la Marne or through the lush Parc de Champagne. These routes offer picturesque views of vineyards, historic châteaux, and natural landscapes, providing a refreshing outdoor experience.

# Getting Around by Taxi and Rental Car

## Taxi Services

While Reims is pedestrian-friendly, taxis are readily available for longer journeys or late-night transportation.

- Taxi Companies: Reliable taxi services such as Allo Taxi Reims and Taxis de la Marne can be booked via phone or hailed at designated taxi stands throughout the city.

### Rental Cars

For travelers seeking flexibility and convenience, renting a car in Reims is an excellent option to explore the Champagne region at your own pace.

- Rental Agencies: Major car rental companies, including Avis, Europcar, and Hertz, have offices conveniently located at Reims Champagne Airport and within the city center.

## Parking in Reims

Parking in Reims is generally accessible, with numerous public parking lots and street parking available throughout the city. Pay attention to parking signs and regulations, especially in restricted zones and during peak hours.

Navigating Reims is a delightful experience, whether you choose to explore its historic quarters on foot, cycle through its scenic streets, or utilize taxi services and rental cars for longer journeys. With its pedestrian-friendly layout, well-developed bike-sharing system, and reliable transportation options, Reims ensures that travelers can effortlessly discover its cultural treasures, culinary delights, and natural beauty. Plan your transportation preferences accordingly to make the most of your visit to this captivating city in the heart of Champagne.

# Chapter 4: Where to Stay inReims

## Luxury Retreats: High-End Hotels

Reims offers luxurious accommodations that cater to discerning travelers seeking comfort, style, and impeccable service.

### L'Assiette Champenoise Hotel

Located in the outskirts of Reims, L'Assiette Champenoise Hotel is a five-star retreat renowned for its elegance and Michelin-starred restaurant. This exclusive hotel offers spacious suites, a serene spa, and personalized concierge services.

- Address: 40 Avenue Paul Vaillant-Couturier, 51430 Tinqueux, France

- Website: [L'Assiette Champenoise Hotel](https://www.assiettechampenoise.com)

## Château Les Crayères

Set within a historic château surrounded by lush gardens, Château Les Crayères offers luxurious rooms and suites decorated in classic French style. Guests can indulge in gourmet dining at the Michelin-starred restaurant or relax with treatments at the spa.

- Address: 64 Boulevard Henry Vasnier, 51100 Reims, France

- Website: [Château Les Crayères](https://www.lescrayeres.com)

# Comfortable Stays: Mid-Range Accommodations

Mid-range hotels in Reims provide comfortable accommodations with modern amenities, ideal for travelers seeking value without compromising on quality.

## Hotel Continental Centre Ville

Located in the heart of Reims, Hotel Continental Centre Ville offers cozy rooms decorated in contemporary style. Guests can enjoy a central location near attractions such as the Cathedral and Place Drouet d'Erlon.

- Address: 93 Place Drouet d'Erlon, 51100 Reims, France
- Website: [Hotel Continental Centre Ville](https://www.hotelcontinental-reims.com)

## Novotel Suites Reims Centre

Novotel Suites Reims Centre provides spacious suites equipped with kitchenettes, perfect for longer stays or families. The hotel features a fitness center, a 24-hour snack bar, and is within walking distance of Reims Opera House.

- Address: 1 Rue Edouard Mignot, 51100 Reims, France

- Website: [Novotel Suites Reims Centre](https://www.accorhotels.com)

# Budget-Friendly Options

For budget-conscious travelers, Reims offers affordable accommodations ranging from hostels to budget hotels.

## Ibis Budget Reims Centre

Ibis Budget Reims Centre provides simple and comfortable rooms at budget-friendly rates. Located near the train station, this hotel offers easy access to public transportation and Reims' main attractions.

- Address: 21 Boulevard Paul Doumer, 51100 Reims, France
- Website: [Ibis Budget Reims Centre](https://www.accorhotels.com)

## Hostellerie La Briqueterie

A charming boutique hotel located in the nearby village of Vinay, Hostellerie La Briqueterie offers cozy rooms with a rustic ambiance. This budget-friendly option provides a peaceful retreat amidst Champagne vineyards.

- Address: 4 Route de Sézanne, 51530 Vinay, France
- Website: [Hostellerie La Briqueterie](https://www.labriqueterie.fr)

# Unique and Boutique Hotels

Reims boasts a selection of unique and boutique hotels, each offering a distinctive charm and personalized experience.

## Hotel de la Paix

Located near the Cathedral, Hotel de la Paix combines Art Deco elegance with modern comforts. This boutique hotel features stylish rooms, a gourmet restaurant, and a rooftop terrace with panoramic views of Reims.

- Address: 9 Rue Buirette, 51100 Reims, France
- Website: [Hotel de la Paix](https://www.bestwestern-lapaix-reims.com)

## Grand Hotel des Templiers

Nestled in a historic mansion, Grand Hotel des Templiers offers luxurious rooms with period furnishings and antique décor. This boutique hotel exudes old-world charm and provides a tranquil oasis in the heart of Reims.

- Address: 22 Rue des Templiers, 51100 Reims, France
- Website: [Grand Hotel des Templiers](https://www.templiers.com)

Whether you're looking for luxury, comfort, affordability, or uniqueness, Reims offers a diverse range of accommodations to suit every traveler's preferences. From luxurious château stays and centrally located hotels to charming boutique options and budget-friendly choices, you'll find the perfect place to rest and rejuvenate during your visit to this enchanting city in Champagne. Choose your ideal accommodation based on location, amenities, and personal style, ensuring a memorable stay in Reims that complements your travel experience.

# Chapter 5: Top Attractions in Reims

## Majestic Reims Cathedral

### Notre-Dame de Reims Cathedral

Notre-Dame de Reims Cathedral stands as a masterpiece of Gothic architecture and is a UNESCO World Heritage site. Known as the "Coronation Cathedral," it has witnessed the coronation of numerous French kings. Marvel at its intricate facade, stunning stained glass windows, and the iconic Smiling Angel sculpture.

- Address: Place du Cardinal Luçon, 51100 Reims, France
- Website: [Notre-Dame de Reims Cathedral](https://www.cathedrale-reims.com)

## Historical Treasures: Palais du Tau and Saint Remi Basilica

### Palais du Tau

Adjacent to the cathedral, Palais du Tau was the former residence of the archbishops of Reims and now serves as a museum. Explore its collection of royal artifacts, including statues, tapestries, and the original treasures used during coronation ceremonies.

- Address: 2 Place du Cardinal Luçon, 51100 Reims, France
- Website: [Palais du Tau](http://www.palais-tau.fr)

## Saint Remi Basilica

Saint Remi Basilica is another architectural gem in Reims, renowned for its Romanesque and Gothic styles. Discover its rich history dating back to the 6th century and admire its impressive stained glass windows and ancient relics.

- Address: Place du Chanoine Ladame, 51100 Reims, France
- Website: [Saint Remi Basilica](https://www.basiliquesaintremi.fr)

## Champagne Houses and Tastings

### Taittinger Champagne House

Experience the art of Champagne-making at Taittinger, one of Reims' prestigious Champagne houses. Tour their historic cellars carved from Roman chalk pits and indulge in tastings of their exquisite Champagnes.

- Address: 9 Place Saint-Nicaise, 51100 Reims, France
- Website: [Taittinger](https://www.taittinger.com)

## Veuve Clicquot Ponsardin

Visit Veuve Clicquot Ponsardin for a guided tour of their extensive cellars and a tasting of their renowned Champagnes, known for their quality and distinctive yellow label.

- Address: 1 Place des Droits de l'Homme, 51100 Reims, France
- Website: [Veuve Clicquot](https://www.veuveclicquot.com)

# Museums of Art and History

## Museum of Fine Arts

Reims' Museum of Fine Arts showcases a diverse collection of artworks spanning from the Middle Ages to the present day. Discover works by renowned artists such as Cranach,

Corot, and Picasso, along with regional treasures and contemporary pieces.

- Address: 8 Rue Chanzy, 51100 Reims, France
- Website: [Museum of Fine Arts](https://musees-reims.fr/fr/musee-des-beaux-arts)

## Musée de la Reddition (Surrender Museum)

Explore the Musée de la Reddition, housed in the former school where the German surrender was signed in 1945. Learn about the end of World War II through exhibits, documents, and artifacts that commemorate this historic event.

- Address: 12 Rue Franklin Roosevelt, 51100 Reims, France
- Website: [Musée de la Reddition](https://www.reims.fr)

Reims captivates visitors with its blend of historical treasures, architectural splendor, and world-class Champagne heritage. From the awe-inspiring Notre-Dame de Reims Cathedral and Palais du Tau to the prestigious Champagne houses and enriching museums, each attraction offers a glimpse into the city's illustrious past and vibrant present. Immerse yourself in Reims' cultural tapestry, and uncover the stories that have shaped this enchanting city in the heart of Champagne.

# Chapter 6: Exploring Reims' Districts

## Old Town Charms: Centre-Ville

### Place Drouet d'Erlon

Centre-Ville is the vibrant heart of Reims, anchored by Place Drouet d'Erlon. This bustling pedestrian square is lined with cafés, shops, and restaurants, making it a hub for dining and entertainment.

**Rue de Vesle**
Parallel to Place Drouet d'Erlon, Rue de Vesle is a bustling shopping street dotted with boutiques, bakeries, and local stores. It's perfect for leisurely strolls and exploring the local culture.

**Notre-Dame de Reims Cathedral**
Centre-Ville is home to the iconic Notre-Dame de Reims Cathedral, a masterpiece of Gothic architecture and a UNESCO World Heritage site. Explore its stunning facade and intricate interiors.

## Artistic Vibes: Quartier Boulingri

### Marché du Boulingrin

Quartier Boulingrin is known for its lively market, Marché du Boulingrin, where locals gather to shop for fresh produce, cheeses, and regional specialties. The market's Art Deco architecture adds to its charm.

**Galerie 36**

Art enthusiasts will appreciate Galerie 36, a contemporary art gallery showcasing works by local and international artists. It's a cultural hotspot within Quartier Boulingrin.

**Cafés and Artisan Shops**
Explore the neighborhood's quaint cafés and artisan shops, where you can sample local delicacies and browse handmade crafts. Quartier Boulingrin offers a blend of creativity and culinary delights.

# Riverside Serenity: Quartier des Capucins

## Promenade de la Suippe

Quartier des Capucins is a tranquil riverside district known for its scenic Promenade de la Suippe. Take a leisurely walk along the riverbanks, enjoying views of lush greenery and historic bridges.

### Parc de la Patte d'Oie
Parc de la Patte d'Oie, located nearby, is a serene park offering a peaceful retreat amidst nature. It's ideal for picnics, jogging, or simply unwinding with beautiful views of the river.

## Historic Bridges

Admire Quartier des Capucins' historic bridges, such as Pont de Vesle and Pont des Tournelles, which connect different parts of Reims and provide picturesque spots for photography.

Reims' districts each offer a unique blend of history, culture, and local charm, inviting visitors to explore their distinctive atmospheres. Whether you're captivated by the Old Town charms of Centre-Ville, inspired by the artistic vibes of Quartier Boulingrin, or seeking riverside serenity in Quartier des Capucins, each district promises unforgettable experiences and hidden gems waiting to be discovered. Embark on a journey through Reims' diverse neighborhoods, and uncover the city's rich tapestry of traditions, artistry, and natural beauty.

# Chapter 7: Immersing in Reims' Culture

## Art Galleries and Creative Spaces

### FRAC Champagne-Ardenne

FRAC Champagne-Ardenne is a contemporary art gallery showcasing temporary exhibitions and installations by emerging and established artists. Located in the former Jesuit College, it offers thought-provoking insights into contemporary art trends.

- Address: 1 Place Museux, 51100 Reims, France
- Website: [FRAC Champagne-Ardenne](http://www.frac-champagneardenne.org)

## Galerie Martine Ehmer

Galerie Martine Ehmer specializes in modern and contemporary art, featuring works by regional and international artists. This gallery is known for its diverse exhibitions and commitment to promoting cultural dialogue through art.

- Address: 16 Rue de l'Université, 51100 Reims, France
- Website: [Galerie Martine Ehmer](https://www.galeriemartineehmer.com)

# Theatrical Performances and Events

## Opéra de Reims

Opéra de Reims hosts a variety of theatrical performances, including opera, ballet, and classical concerts. The historic theater's ornate architecture and acoustics provide a perfect setting for cultural performances.

- Address: 3-5 Rue Chanzy, 51100 Reims, France
- Website: [Opéra de Reims](https://www.operadereims.com)

## La Comédie de Reims

La Comédie de Reims is a contemporary theater that stages innovative plays, performances, and experimental productions. It's a hub for creative expression and cultural exploration in Reims.

- Address: 3 Chaussée Bocquaine, 51100 Reims, France
- Website: [La Comédie de Reims](https://www.lacomediedereims.fr)

# Festivals and Cultural Celebrations

## Fêtes Johanniques

Fêtes Johanniques celebrates Reims' historical significance as the city where Joan of Arc participated in the coronation of Charles VII. This annual festival includes medieval reenactments, parades, and cultural events honoring Joan of Arc's legacy.

- Dates: May
- Location: Various venues in Reims

## Festival Flâneries Musicales

Festival Flâneries Musicales de Reims is a renowned music festival featuring classical concerts, chamber music, and recitals held in historic venues throughout Reims. It attracts internationally acclaimed musicians and music enthusiasts from around the world.

- Dates: June-July
- Location: Various venues in Reims

Immersing yourself in Reims' culture offers a rich tapestry of artistic expression, theatrical performances, and vibrant festivals. From contemporary art galleries like FRAC Champagne-Ardenne to cultural landmarks such as Opéra de Reims and annual festivals like Fêtes Johanniques and Festival Flâneries Musicales, Reims invites you to explore its dynamic cultural scene and participate in memorable cultural experiences. Delve into the city's artistic heritage, attend captivating performances, and join in lively celebrations that celebrate Reims' cultural vitality and historical significance.

# Chapter 8: Outdoor Adventures Around Reims

# Champagne Vineyards and Tours

# Champagne Tasting Tours

Explore the scenic Champagne vineyards surrounding Reims with guided tours that offer insights into the region's prestigious winemaking heritage. Visit renowned Champagne houses and boutique wineries to sample their exquisite blends and learn about the production process.

## Recommended Tours:

**Champagne Pommery**: Discover the historic cellars of Pommery and enjoy tastings of their renowned Champagnes.

- Address: 5 Place du Général Gouraud, 51100 Reims, France
- Website: [Champagne Pommery](https://www.champagnepommery.com)

**Champagne Taittinger**: Tour the Taittinger cellars carved from Roman chalk pits and savor their distinctive Champagnes.

- Address: 9 Place Saint-Nicaise, 51100 Reims, France
- Website: [Champagne Taittinger](https://www.taittinger.com)

# Parks, Gardens, and Green Spaces

## Parc de Champagne

Parc de Champagne is a sprawling green oasis where visitors can relax amidst manicured lawns, tranquil ponds, and picturesque walking paths. It's an ideal spot for picnics, leisurely strolls, and enjoying scenic views of Reims' skyline.

- Address: Avenue du Général Giraud, 51100 Reims, France

## Jardin des Secrets

Jardin des Secrets is a charming botanical garden showcasing a diverse collection of plants, flowers, and sculptures. Wander through themed sections such as the rose garden and Japanese garden, offering serene retreats within the city.

- Address: 2 Rue des Fuseliers, 51100 Reims, France

64

# Sports and Recreation Activities

## Golf de Reims

Golf enthusiasts can tee off at Golf de Reims, a prestigious golf course surrounded by Champagne vineyards. Enjoy a round of golf amidst scenic landscapes and rolling hills.

- Address: 8 Chemin de Fresne, 51100 Reims, France
- Website: [Golf de Reims](https://www.golfdereims.com)

## Canoeing on the Marne River

Embark on a canoeing adventure along the Marne River, offering picturesque views of vineyards, historic villages, and natural landscapes. Canoe rental services are available for exploring the tranquil waters at your own pace.

- Location: Marne River, near Reims

Outdoor adventures around Reims offer a blend of cultural exploration and natural beauty, from Champagne vineyard tours and tastings to serene parks, gardens, and recreational activities. Whether you're indulging in Champagne experiences, exploring lush green spaces, or enjoying outdoor sports like golf and canoeing, Reims provides diverse opportunities to connect with its scenic surroundings and vibrant outdoor lifestyle. Plan your outdoor adventures to discover the charm and natural wonders of this enchanting city nestled in the heart of Champagne.

# Chapter 9: Shopping in Reims

## Local Markets and Specialty Stores

### Marché du Boulingrin

Marché du Boulingrin is a vibrant market offering fresh produce, cheeses, meats, and local specialties. It's a favorite spot among locals and visitors alike for sampling regional delicacies and experiencing the lively atmosphere of a traditional French market.

- Address: Place du Boulingrin, 51100 Reims, France

### Les Halles du Boulingrin

Les Halles du Boulingrin is an indoor market housed in an Art Deco building, featuring stalls selling fresh fruits, vegetables, seafood, and gourmet products. It's an ideal place to shop for quality ingredients and artisanal treats.

- Address: Place du Boulingrin, 51100 Reims, France

## Boutique Shopping and Designer Finds

## Rue de Vesle

Rue de Vesle is Reims' main shopping street, lined with a mix of international brands, designer boutiques, and specialty shops. Explore its fashion stores, jewelry shops, and stylish boutiques for unique finds and designer labels.

**Boulevard Lundy**
Boulevard Lundy offers a sophisticated shopping experience with upscale boutiques and chic stores. From fashion and accessories to home decor and gourmet delicacies, it caters to discerning shoppers seeking quality and style.

# Shopping Centers for Every Need

## Centre Commercial Espace d'Erlon
Centre Commercial Espace d'Erlon is a modern shopping center located in the heart of Reims, offering a diverse range

of shops, restaurants, and entertainment options. It's convenient for everything from fashion shopping to dining and leisure activities.

- Address: 20 Rue Buirette, 51100 Reims, France

## Parc Commercial Cernay

Parc Commercial Cernay is a retail park on the outskirts of Reims, featuring large stores, supermarkets, and specialty shops. It's ideal for convenient shopping with ample parking and a variety of retail offerings.

- Address: Rue Louis Blériot, 51420 Cernay-lès-Reims, France

Shopping in Reims promises a delightful blend of local markets brimming with fresh produce and gourmet treats, boutique shopping offering designer finds and unique souvenirs, and modern shopping centers catering to every need. Whether you're exploring traditional markets like Marché du Boulingrin, browsing fashionable boutiques on Rue de Vesle, or enjoying a shopping spree at Centre Commercial Espace d'Erlon, Reims offers diverse shopping experiences that reflect its cultural richness and contemporary flair. Discover the city's vibrant shopping scene, and indulge in retail therapy amidst the charm of this historic Champagne capital.

# Chapter 10: Dining and Cuisine in Reims

# Gastronomic Delights: Regional Cuisine

## Bouchon des Filles

Experience traditional French cuisine with a modern twist at Bouchon des Filles. This cozy bistro showcases seasonal dishes crafted from local ingredients, accompanied by a selection of wines from the Champagne region.

- Address: 10 Rue des Fossés Saint-Jacques, 51100 Reims, France
- Website: [Bouchon des Filles](https://www.bouchondesfilles.com)

# Le Foch

Le Foch offers refined interpretations of regional specialties in an elegant setting. Indulge in dishes like escargots, coq au vin, and crème brûlée, paired with a curated list of Champagnes and wines.

- Address: 37 Boulevard Foch, 51100 Reims, France
- Website: [Le Foch](http://www.restaurantlefoch.com)

# Champagne Pairings and Tastings

## Les Crayères

Les Crayères is renowned for its exceptional dining experience and extensive Champagne selection. Enjoy gourmet cuisine paired with prestigious Champagnes in a luxurious setting within a historic château.

- Address: 64 Boulevard Henry Vasnier, 51100 Reims, France
- Website: [Les Crayères](https://www.lescrayeres.com)

## Caves du Forum

Caves du Forum offers an intimate wine bar atmosphere perfect for Champagne tastings. Discover a variety of Champagnes by the glass or bottle, accompanied by charcuterie and cheese boards.

- Address: 8 Rue de Mars, 51100 Reims, France
- Website: [Caves du Forum](https://www.cavesduforum.com)

# Fine Dining Experiences

## Assiette Champenoise

Assiette Champenoise boasts three Michelin stars for its innovative cuisine and impeccable service. Chef Arnaud Lallement showcases seasonal flavors and local ingredients in dishes that elevate French gastronomy.

- Address: 40 Avenue Paul Vaillant-Couturier, 51430 Tinqueux, France
- Website: [Assiette Champenoise](https://www.assiettechampenoise.com)

## L'Alambic

L'Alambic offers a refined dining experience in the heart of Reims, featuring a creative menu that highlights contemporary French cuisine. Pair your meal with a selection of fine wines and Champagnes.

- Address: 2 Rue des Élus, 51100 Reims, France
- Website: [L'Alambic](https://www.lalambic-reims.fr)

# Cozy Cafés and Bistros

## Café du Palais

Located near the Reims Cathedral, Café du Palais offers a cozy ambiance and a menu of French classics, pastries, and artisanal coffees. It's perfect for a relaxing break during your exploration of the city.

- Address: 14 Place Myron Herrick, 51100 Reims, France
- Website: [Café du Palais](https://www.cafedupalais-reims.fr)

## Le Gaulois

Le Gaulois is a charming bistro known for its warm atmosphere and traditional French dishes. Enjoy a casual meal of quiche Lorraine, salads, and homemade desserts, accompanied by a glass of Champagne.

- Address: 54 Rue de Mars, 51100 Reims, France

- Website: [Le Gaulois](https://www.legaulois-reims.fr)

Dining in Reims offers a delectable journey through regional cuisine, Champagne pairings, fine dining experiences, and cozy café atmospheres. Whether you're savoring traditional dishes at Bouchon des Filles, indulging in Champagne tastings at Les Crayères, experiencing Michelin-starred excellence at Assiette Champenoise, or enjoying a relaxed meal at Café du Palais, Reims' culinary scene promises unforgettable flavors and memorable dining experiences. Explore the city's gastronomic heritage and vibrant café culture, and discover why Reims is a destination where every meal is a celebration of French culinary artistry.

# Chapter 11: Nightlife and Entertainment

# Bars and Pubs: Local Hotspots

## Le Coq Rouge

Le Coq Rouge is a popular bar known for its cozy atmosphere and extensive selection of beers, wines, and cocktails. Enjoy live music performances and friendly ambiance in this lively venue.

- Address: 42 Rue de Mars, 51100 Reims, France
- Website: [Le Coq Rouge](https://www.lecoqrouge-reims.fr)

## Café du Palais

Café du Palais transforms into a vibrant bar in the evenings, offering a relaxed setting near the Reims Cathedral. Sip on local wines or enjoy classic cocktails while soaking in the historic surroundings.

- Address: 14 Place Myron Herrick, 51100 Reims, France
- Website: [Café du Palais](https://www.cafedupalais-reims.fr)

# Nightclubs for Dancing

### La Cartonnerie

La Cartonnerie is Reims' premier nightclub venue, hosting DJ sets, themed parties, and live music events. Dance the night away in this dynamic space known for its energetic atmosphere and eclectic music lineup.

- Address: 84 Rue du Docteur Lemoine, 51100 Reims, France
- Website: [La Cartonnerie](https://www.lacartonnerie.fr)

**Le Safari Club**
Le Safari Club offers a lively nightclub experience with multiple dance floors, VIP lounges, and a variety of music genres. It's a popular spot among locals and visitors looking to party into the early hours.

- Address: 20 Rue de Mars, 51100 Reims, France
- Website: [Le Safari Club](https://www.lesafariclub-reims.fr)

# Live Music Venues

## La Comédie de Reims

La Comédie de Reims not only hosts theatrical performances but also occasional live music concerts featuring local and international artists. Check their schedule for upcoming musical events in this cultural venue.

- Address: 3 Chaussée Bocquaine, 51100 Reims, France
- Website: [La Comédie de Reims](https://www.lacomediedereims.fr)

## Le Temps des Cerises

Le Temps des Cerises is a cozy bar known for its intimate atmosphere and live music sessions, ranging from jazz and blues to acoustic performances. Enjoy a relaxing evening with great music and a laid-back vibe.

- Address: 10 Rue de Tambour, 51100 Reims, France
- Website: [Le Temps des Cerises](https://www.letempsdescerises-reims.fr)

# Cultural Evenings and Events

## Palais du Tau

Palais du Tau hosts occasional cultural events, including exhibitions, lectures, and special performances. It's a historic venue near the Reims Cathedral, offering unique cultural experiences throughout the year.

- Address: 2 Place du Cardinal Luçon, 51100 Reims, France
- Website: [Palais du Tau](https://www.palais-du-tau.fr)

## Festival Flâneries Musicales de Reims

Festival Flâneries Musicales de Reims not only features classical music concerts during the day but also offers evening performances in various venues across the city. Immerse yourself in the city's cultural scene during this annual festival.

- Dates: June-July
- Location: Various venues in Reims

Reims' nightlife and entertainment scene offers a vibrant mix of bars, nightclubs, live music venues, and cultural events, ensuring there's something for everyone to enjoy after dark. Whether you're exploring local hotspots like Le Coq Rouge and La Cartonnerie, dancing the night away at Le Safari Club, discovering live music at La Comédie de Reims and Le Temps des Cerises, or attending cultural evenings at Palais du Tau and festivals like Flâneries Musicales, Reims promises unforgettable nights filled with excitement and cultural richness. Experience the city's lively nightlife, and discover why Reims is a destination where the fun continues long after the sun sets.

# Chapter 12: Day Trips from Reims

## Epernay: Capital of Champagne

## Avenue de Champagne

Epernay, known as the capital of Champagne, is a short drive from Reims and offers a luxurious experience along its prestigious Avenue de Champagne. Explore renowned Champagne houses like Moët & Chandon, Perrier-Jouët, and Mercier, where you can tour their cellars and indulge in tastings of their finest Champagnes.

- Distance from Reims: Approximately 25 kilometers southeast
- Website: [Avenue de Champagne](https://www.avenue-de-champagne.com)

# Charming Villages of Montagne de Reims

## Verzy

Explore the picturesque villages nestled in the Montagne de Reims regional park, known for their quaint charm and scenic vineyard landscapes. Visit Verzy, famous for its twisted beech trees and hiking trails offering panoramic views of the Champagne countryside.

- Distance from Reims: Various villages within a 30-minute drive
- Website: [Montagne de Reims Regional Park](https://www.parc-montagnedereims.fr)

# Historical Sites: Verdun and Laon

## Verdun

Step back in time with a visit to Verdun, a historic town known for its significant role during World War I. Explore the Verdun Memorial and battlefield sites, where you can pay homage to fallen soldiers and gain insights into the Great War's impact on the region.

- Distance from Reims: Approximately 90 kilometers southwest

- Website: [Verdun Memorial](https://www.verdunmemorial.eu)

## Laon

Discover the medieval town of Laon, perched atop a hill with its iconic cathedral and well-preserved ramparts. Stroll through the cobbled streets lined with half-timbered houses, visit the Cathedral of Notre-Dame, and enjoy panoramic views from the city's ancient ramparts.

- Distance from Reims: Approximately 50 kilometers northeast
- Website: [Laon Tourism](https://www.tourisme-paysdelaon.com)

Day trips from Reims offer a diverse range of experiences, from exploring the Champagne capital of Epernay along the Avenue de Champagne to discovering the charming villages of Montagne de Reims and exploring historical sites like Verdun and Laon. Whether you're fascinated by Champagne heritage, picturesque landscapes, or medieval history, these day trips provide enriching opportunities to explore beyond Reims and delve into the cultural and natural treasures of the Champagne region. Plan your excursions and discover the allure of these nearby destinations that complement your visit to Reims with unique and memorable experiences.

# Chapter 13: Family-Friendly Activities

## Museums and Interactive Exhibits

### Musée Automobile Reims-Champagne

Explore the Musée Automobile Reims-Champagne, where vintage cars and classic automobiles are on display. This family-friendly museum offers interactive exhibits and workshops that appeal to both children and adults interested in automotive history.

- Address: 84 Avenue Georges Clemenceau, 51100 Reims, France
- Website: [Musée Automobile Reims-Champagne](https://www.musee-automobile-reims-champagne.com)

## Planétarium de Reims

Visit the Planétarium de Reims for an educational and entertaining experience exploring the wonders of astronomy. The planetarium offers shows and exhibitions that engage visitors of all ages in learning about the cosmos.

- Address: 31 Boulevard Pommery, 51100 Reims, France
- Website: [Planétarium de Reims](https://www.reims.fr/planetarium)

# Parks, Playgrounds, and Picnic Spots

## Parc de la Patte d'Oie

Parc de la Patte d'Oie is a sprawling park ideal for family outings, featuring playgrounds, picnic areas, and scenic walking trails. Enjoy recreational activities amidst lush greenery and serene surroundings.

- Address: Avenue François Mauriac, 51100 Reims, France

## Jardin d'Horticulture

Jardin d'Horticulture is a botanical garden offering a peaceful retreat with diverse plant species, themed gardens, and open spaces for picnics and leisurely walks. It's a tranquil spot for families to relax and enjoy nature.

- Address: 19 Rue Buirette, 51100 Reims, France

# Educational Tours and Workshops

## Champagne Tasting Workshops

Many Champagne houses, such as Veuve Clicquot and Taittinger, offer educational tours and workshops tailored for families. Children can learn about the Champagne-making process while adults indulge in tastings of Champagne varieties.

## Various Champagne houses in Reims
### Basilique Saint-Remi

Visit the Basilique Saint-Remi, a UNESCO World Heritage site, for guided tours that cater to families. Explore the historic church and learn about its significance in Reims' history through interactive tours and educational exhibits.

- Address: Place Saint-Remi, 51100 Reims, France
- Website: [Basilique Saint-Remi](https://www.reims-tourism.com/basilica-of-saint-remi)

Reims offers a variety of family-friendly activities, from exploring interactive museums like Musée Automobile Reims-Champagne and learning about astronomy at Planétarium de Reims to enjoying outdoor adventures at Parc de la Patte d'Oie and educational tours at Champagne houses and historic sites. Whether you're discovering the city's cultural heritage, exploring botanical gardens, or participating in Champagne tasting workshops, Reims provides engaging experiences that cater to families looking to enjoy quality time together. Plan your family-friendly itinerary and create lasting memories in this captivating city at the heart of the Champagne region.

# Chapter 14: Practical Information for Visitors

## Tourist Information Centers

### Office de Tourisme de Reims

The Office de Tourisme de Reims is your go-to resource for information on attractions, events, tours, and accommodations in Reims. Friendly staff can provide maps, brochures, and personalized recommendations to enhance your visit.

- Address: 6 Rue Rockefeller, 51100 Reims, France
- Contact: +33 3 26 77 45 00
- Website: [Office de Tourisme de Reims](https://www.reims-tourism.com)

## Emergency Contacts

### Emergency Services

In case of emergencies, dial the European emergency number: 112.

#### Police

For non-emergency police assistance or to report incidents:

- **Police Station**: 14 Rue Carnot, 51100 Reims, France
- **Contact**: +33 3 26 85 50 50

**Medical Emergencies**

For medical emergencies or ambulance services:

- **Emergency Medical Services**: Dial 15

# Local Etiquette and Customs

## Greetings

When meeting someone in Reims, a handshake and a polite "Bonjour" (good morning/afternoon) are customary. In more informal settings, such as among friends, a kiss on each cheek may be exchanged.

**Dining Etiquette**

In restaurants, it's customary to wait to be seated and to say "Bonjour" to the server upon entering. Tipping is appreciated but not obligatory, as service charges are often included in the bill.

**Cultural Sensitivity**

Respect local customs and cultural practices, especially when visiting religious sites or participating in cultural events. Dress modestly when entering churches and other religious venues.

Understanding practical information such as tourist information centers for guidance, emergency contacts for assistance, and local etiquette and customs for respectful interactions will enhance your experience in Reims. Whether seeking travel advice, needing emergency services, or navigating cultural norms, being informed ensures a smooth and enjoyable visit to this historic city in the heart of Champagne. Embrace the local customs, engage with the community, and make the most of your time exploring Reims' rich cultural heritage and vibrant atmosphere.

# Chapter 15: Travel Tips for Reims

# Best Times to Visit

Reims is charming year-round, but the best times to visit are during the spring (April to June) and autumn (September to October) months. These seasons offer pleasant weather, fewer crowds, and vibrant landscapes of vineyards in bloom or adorned with autumn colors. Summer (July to August) can be busy with tourists, while winter (December to February) brings colder temperatures but festive Christmas markets.

# Safety Tips and Advice

- General Safety: Reims is generally a safe city, but it's advisable to remain vigilant in crowded areas and to safeguard personal belongings, especially in tourist hotspots.
- Emergency Numbers: For emergencies, dial 112 for European emergency services. For non-emergency police assistance, contact the local police station at +33 3 26 85 50 50.
- Healthcare: Familiarize yourself with the location of hospitals and pharmacies. Medical emergencies can be addressed by dialing 15 for ambulance services.

# Budget Planning Tips

- Accommodations: Reims offers a range of accommodations, from luxury hotels to budget-friendly options like hostels and guesthouses. Booking in advance, especially during peak seasons, can secure better rates.

- Dining: Enjoy local cuisine at affordable prices by exploring neighborhood bistros and cafes. Many restaurants offer prix-fixe menus at lunchtime, providing a budget-friendly dining option.
- Transportation: Opt for walking or cycling within the city center, where attractions are easily accessible. Public buses and trams offer affordable options for longer distances, and renting a car can be economical for exploring the Champagne region.

## Eco-Friendly Travel Practices

- Public Transportation: Utilize Reims' efficient public transportation system, including buses and trams, to reduce carbon footprint while exploring the city.
- Cycling and Walking: Embrace eco-friendly modes of transport by renting bicycles or exploring Reims on foot, which allows you to appreciate the city's architecture and green spaces.
- Waste Reduction: Support local businesses that promote sustainability by reducing single-use plastics and opting for reusable products during your stay.

By choosing the best times to visit, practicing safety precautions, budgeting wisely, and adopting eco-friendly travel practices, you can enhance your experience in Reims while minimizing environmental impact. Whether exploring historic landmarks, enjoying local cuisine, or indulging in Champagne tastings, thoughtful planning ensures a memorable and responsible visit to this captivating city in the heart of Champagne.

# Chapter 16: Reims for Business Travelers

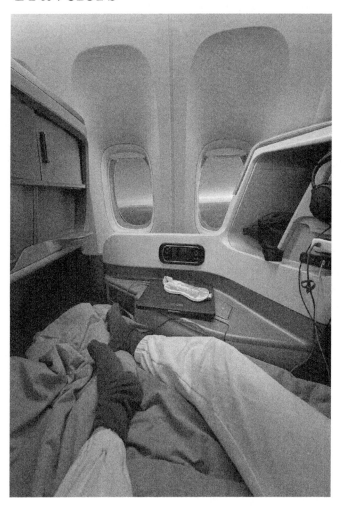

# Conference Venues and Meeting Spaces

## Centre des Congrès de Reims

The Centre des Congrès de Reims offers modern conference facilities equipped with state-of-the-art technology. It hosts a variety of events, including conferences, seminars, and trade shows, accommodating large gatherings with ease.

- Address: 12 Boulevard du Général Leclerc, 51100 Reims, France
- Website: [Centre des Congrès de Reims](https://www.reims-congres.com)

## Domaine Pommery

Domaine Pommery provides unique meeting spaces within its historic Champagne cellars. Ideal for corporate events and private gatherings, it offers a distinctive setting surrounded by centuries-old Champagne traditions.

- Address: 5 Place du Général Gouraud, 51100 Reims, France
- Website: [Domaine Pommery](https://www.domaine-pommery.com)

# Business Services and Amenities

## Business Hotels

Choose from a range of business-friendly hotels in Reims, offering amenities such as high-speed internet, business centers, meeting rooms, and concierge services. Recommended options include:

## Hôtel de la Paix

- Address: 9 Rue Buirette, 51100 Reims, France
- Website: [Hôtel de la Paix](https://www.hotel-lapaix-reims.com)

**Novotel Suites Reims Centre**
- Address: 1 Rue Edouard Mignot, 51100 Reims, France
- Website: [Novotel Suites Reims Centre](https://www.accorhotels.com/gb/hotel-7238-novotel-suites-reims-centre/index.shtml)

# Networking Opportunities

## Reims Chamber of Commerce and Industry

The Reims Chamber of Commerce and Industry (CCI) organizes networking events, workshops, and business forums throughout the year. It's a valuable resource for connecting with local professionals and exploring business opportunities in the region.

- Address: 5 Rue des Marmouzets, 51100 Reims, France
- Website: [Reims CCI](https://www.reims.cci.fr)

## Professional Networking Groups

Join local professional networking groups, such as Réseau Entreprendre Champagne Ardenne, to expand your business contacts and engage with like-minded entrepreneurs in Reims.

Reims offers excellent facilities and opportunities for business travelers, from modern conference venues like Centre des

Congrès de Reims and unique settings at Domaine Pommery to business-friendly hotels and networking opportunities provided by the Reims Chamber of Commerce and professional groups. Whether attending conferences, hosting meetings, or exploring networking events, Reims combines business efficiency with cultural charm, ensuring a productive and enjoyable experience for business travelers in the heart of the Champagne region.

# Chapter 17: Conclusion

## Reflecting on Your Reims Experience

As you conclude your journey through Reims, take a moment to reflect on the rich tapestry of history, culture, and Champagne that defines this captivating city. From its majestic cathedral to the tranquil vineyards of Champagne, Reims offers a blend of ancient grandeur and vibrant modernity that leaves a lasting impression.

## Souvenirs and Memories to Take Home

- Champagne: Indulge in bottles of world-renowned Champagne from local producers like Taittinger, Veuve Clicquot, or Pommery, ensuring your memories of Reims linger with every celebratory toast.

- Local Delicacies: Treat yourself to regional specialties such as pink biscuits, mustard from Reims, or locally crafted chocolates, perfect for sharing a taste of Reims with friends and family.

- Art and Crafts: Explore boutiques and galleries in Quartier Boulingrin for unique artworks, artisanal crafts, and designer souvenirs that capture the essence of Reims' creative spirit.

## Planning Your Return to Reims

As you bid farewell to Reims, consider when you'll return to continue your exploration of this dynamic city and its surrounding Champagne region. Whether revisiting favorite landmarks, delving deeper into cultural experiences, or embarking on new adventures, Reims eagerly awaits your return with open arms.

Reims is more than a destination; it's a journey through time, taste, and tradition. From the striking silhouette of its cathedral to the effervescent allure of Champagne, every moment spent in Reims enriches the soul and creates memories to cherish. Whether you've come for its historical treasures, culinary delights, or business opportunities, Reims leaves an indelible mark, inviting you to return and discover even more of its hidden treasures and vibrant charms. Until next time, may your memories of Reims sparkle like the bubbles in a glass of its finest Champagne.

Printed in Great Britain
by Amazon